HEAVEN HELP ME THROUGH ANOTHER DAY!

Inspired by Faith

Heaven Help Me Through Another Day!
ISBN 978-0-9853005-2-4

Published by Product Concept Mfg., Inc.
2175 N. Academy Circle #200, Colorado Springs, CO 80909

©2012 Product Concept Mfg., Inc. All rights reserved.

Written and Compiled by Patricia Mitchell
in association with Product Concept Mfg., Inc.

All scripture quotations are from the King James version
of the Bible unless otherwise noted.

Scriptures taken from the Holy Bible,
New International Version®, NIV®.
Copyright © 1973, 1978, 1984 by Biblica, Inc.™
Used by permission of Zondervan.
All rights reserved worldwide.
www.zondervan.com

Sayings not having a credit listed are contributed by writers
for Product Concept Mfg., Inc. or in a rare case,
the author is unknown.

HEAVEN HELP ME THROUGH ANOTHER DAY!

Heaven is under our feet as well as over our heads.

Henry David Thoreau

It's hard to underestimate the healing power of humor. After all, laughter isn't called the "best medicine" for nothing! It makes almost any pill a little easier to swallow.

Heaven Help Me is a collection of uplifting devotions on topics from A to Z. Each reflection comes with witty and positive sayings and quotes, reminding you that, by the grace of Heaven, you really will make it through the day!

A merry heart doeth good like a medicine.

Proverbs 17:22

ANXIETY

...shoo!

Knock, knock! Who's there? Why, it's Anxiety right on your doorstep! If you're like most of us, you open the door and let her in. And she stays. And stays. And stays.

Whether anxiety stems from niggling concerns or a full-blown crisis, why not introduce her to God? Talk to Him about her. You might be surprised how fast He shows Anxiety out the door. Then you'll have your living room (and mind) free to entertain happier comers, like Optimism. Confidence. Good Feelings.

Knock, knock! Who's there?

The birds of anxiety may fly over
your head, but you don't have to let
them roost in your hair.
Proverb

Blessed is the person who is too busy
to worry in the daytime and too sleepy
to worry at night.

Drag your thoughts away from your
troubles...by the ears, by the heels,
or any other way you can manage it.
Mark Twain

My life has been full of terrible
misfortunes, most of which
never happened.
Montaigne

Instead of newspaper headlines,
read advice columns, where the most
anxiety-producing issues concern
children's table manners.

Today is the tomorrow you were chewing
your nails about yesterday.

BELIEVE
...it makes
a difference.

Say you walk outside believing you'll be struck by lightning. In all probability, you're not going to get zapped; but it's possible you'll trip and break a leg while you're gawking skyward!

Believe God loves you, not only because He does, but because what you believe really matters. Holding firmly to His love, you'll walk anywhere expecting God's blessings, God's goodness, God's excellent plans unfolding for you.

Positive, uplifting, and true beliefs keep you strolling in the sunshine all day long.

A pediatrician wanted to put her young patients at ease during their checkups. Before listening to their chest, she would fit the stethoscope into their ears and let them hear the sound of their own heart. She loved to see their eyes widen in awe.

"Listen," she said to one little girl, "what do you think that tap-tap-tap sound is?"

The girl listened thoughtfully, and then she brightened up and exclaimed, "It must be Jesus knocking!"

A Christian was thrown into the arena with a hungry lion. Terrified, the man fell on his knees and begged God to spare his life. As he was speaking, the lion, too, got down on his knees and began to pray.

On seeing this, the Christian threw his hands in the air and immediately launched into a hymn of gratitude and praise. "Shush!" the lion said in rebuke. "I'm saying grace."

Contrary to popular belief, it wasn't the apple on the tree that got us kicked out of Eden— it was the pair on the ground.

CRISES
...they keep life interesting.

A crisis flares up, and a flock of fixers and spin doctors are all over it like ducks on a snail. Rarely do they succeed at anything except extending the damage.

Crises blaze pretty much out of your control (assuming the cause of the crisis isn't you). A few damp towels thrown at them might help smother the flames, though–composure, a cool head, and a considered response. Deep breaths, too, as long as you're not standing in the line of smoke.

And look at it this way: A crisis a day keeps boredom at bay.

Any idiot can face a crisis—it's this
day-to-day living that wears you out.
Anton Chekhov

A problem shared is attention gained.

In any time of trouble, there's a light at
the end of the tunnel. Just pray it isn't an
oncoming train.

It just wouldn't be a picnic
without the ants.

If you can keep your head when all about
you are losing theirs, you probably have
no idea what's going on.

Life is 10 percent what you make it,
and 90 percent how you take it.
Irving Berlin

Sometimes the smallest things
are the hardest to take. For instance,
you can sit on a mountain more
comfortably than on a tack.

CRITICISM

...you can
count on it.

As long as you're living and breathing, you can count on critics carping from the sidelines (and sometimes right in front of your face).

The only one who knows your heart better than you do is God, and He's not a sour-faced critic. He's a loving guide and compassionate counselor. Through the wise advice of others, as well as meditation, prayer, and the application of Scripture, you discover the choices right for you.

Let fault-finders fuss as they may. When you know you're doing the right thing, keep on doing it.

Any fool can criticize, condemn and
complain, and most fools do.
Benjamin Franklin

Don't criticize someone until you've
walked a mile in her shoes;
and by that time you'll be a mile away
and have her shoes.

Remember, a statue has never been
set up in honor of a critic!
Jean Sibelius

God created the world,
and then the critics showed up.

If you hear that someone is
speaking ill of you, instead of trying to
defend yourself, you should say:
"He obviously does not know me very
well, since there are so many other
faults he could have mentioned."
Epictetus

One mustn't criticize other people
on grounds where he can't stand
perpendicular himself.
Mark Twain

DREAMS
...why waste time with small ones?

Some people dream of becoming a star athlete, famous actor, or powerful CEO. Others among us harbor less lofty ambitions, such as actually having an hour left over at the end of the day for a soaker bubble bath.

Your dreams express your heart's desires–kind of like what you would do if you ran the world. And while some of your aspirations might appear unrealistic, don't dismiss them. Within each one there lies the glimmer of an idea you can probably make happen.

Just a dream? Ask God–the one who, after all, does run the world!

If your dreams are turning to dust…
vacuum.

Last night I got a double rest.
I dreamed I was sleeping.

Start by doing the necessary,
then the possible, and suddenly
you are doing the impossible.
Francis of Assisi

He who hesitates is not only lost,
but miles from the next exit.

Twenty years from now you will be more
disappointed by the things that you didn't
do than by the ones you did do. So throw
off the bowlines. Sail away from the safe
harbor. Catch the trade winds in your
sails. Explore. Dream. Discover.
Mark Twain

EXERCISE
...do I *have* to?

There are more reasons to stay in a chair than to get off it. You're at the computer, and you're obliged to sit. Or you've been standing all day, and your legs hurt. Or you just plain like to sit.

To many of us, exercise is a bad word, but we have to admit it's good for us. It gets blood circulating, heart pumping, and muscles stretching. So maybe we should change what we call it. From now on, it's a chair vacation, a vertical adventure, or quality time with our lungs and elbows.

Anything but *exercise*.

Exercise the smart way—start slowly,
and then taper off from there.

Go to any bookstore—you'll find diet
and exercise books right in front,
located between humor and fiction.

I'm pushing sixty.
That is exercise enough for me.
Mark Twain

Exercise is a dirty word.
Every time I say it,
I wash out my mouth with chocolate.

An elderly couple arrived together at the Pearly Gates. St. Peter invited them into heaven, and led them to their forever home—a beautifully appointed mansion surrounded by a lush garden, fully stocked fishing pond, and manicured golf course. They were overjoyed.

Once Peter left them and they were alone, the man turned to his wife and frowned. "You know, Clara," he said, "we could have had all this twenty years ago if you hadn't insisted we give up junk food and go to the gym every day!"

FRIENDS

...can't live without them (and wouldn't want to, either).

Where would you be without your friends? Possibly right where you are, but having a lot less fun.

Yes, it's wonderful to hear toddler Meggie say the cutest thing you've ever heard, but even better to share her brilliant utterance with a friend. Same is true when you get a promotion, or plan a cruise, or find the perfect purse–half (or more) of the fun is telling your very best friend all about it.

Sure, you'd be someplace without your friends, but it's no place you'd really want to hang out for long.

Friendship is like a bank account.
You can't continue to draw on it
without making deposits.

A friend is someone who, when you're
acting like a fool, doesn't believe the
condition is permanent.

If social networking sites suddenly
disappeared, how would we know
who our friends are?

Only true friends will tell you
when your face is dirty.

I don't need a friend who changes when I
change and who nods when I nod;
my shadow does that much better.
Plutarch

If my friends were to jump off a cliff,
I wouldn't jump with them—
I'd be at the bottom ready to catch them.

GOODNESS
...gracious!

If you think you're being taken for granted, imagine how God feels! Yet His blessings come to each one of us every day with or without our asking. So why take the trouble to ask?

Because in our asking, we remind ourselves where our blessings come from. Our requests to Him acknowledge His work in our life, and they express our reliance on Him.

Yes, He is now and will remain the source of all you have, but it's a good thing to put God's truth in words.

If your brow is wrinkled with worry,
come to God for a faith lift.

There is a God-shaped
vacuum in every heart.
Blaise Pascal

Those who kneel before God
can stand before anyone.

Most people want to serve God,
but only in an advisory capacity.

God may postpone,
but He doesn't overlook.

Funny how long it feels to sit in church
for an hour, but how quickly a team plays
sixty minutes of basketball.

GRATITUDE

...it's a state
of mind.

If your childhood birthdays and Christmases were followed by an afternoon of enforced thank-you-note writing, good! If not, there's still time to get into the thank-you habit.

But before you pull out pen and paper (yes, we're talking snail-mail), think about where true gratitude begins. It's not a reaction to receiving a present, but a response from an appreciative heart.

An appreciative heart needs no prompting when it comes to thanking the one who gave that thoughtfully chosen gift...kindly offered help... consistently caring advice...lovingly created world.

"Grateful?" whined a woman to her friend, "what have I got to be grateful for? I have a mountain of overdue bills in front of me!" "Well," her friend ventured, "you can be very grateful you're not one of your creditors."

Gratitude is a vaccine, an antitoxin, and an antiseptic.
John Henry Jowett

If the only prayer you said in your whole
life was "thank you," that would suffice.
Meister Eckhart

Gratitude is the best attitude.

When we were children we were
grateful to those who filled our
stockings at Christmas time.
Why are we not grateful to God
for filling our stockings with legs?
G. K. Chesterton

HAPPINESS

...grab some for yourself.

Happy? For most people, the answer lies somewhere between "yes" and "no." Though you haven't achieved perfect bliss, you must admit that there are some things in your life you wouldn't trade for a million dollars (well, maybe not for a *million*…).

Happiness isn't a denial of sadness, just a realization that both happiness and sadness are part of life. We can focus on one or the other, either lifting our mood to the treetops with what's good, or beating down our mood into the ground with what's bad.

Choose which way you want to go.

Show me an optimist,
and I'll show you a happy-chondriac.

Some cause happiness wherever they go;
others whenever they go.
Oscar Wilde

How did Jonah feel when the big fish
swallowed him?
Down in the mouth, of course!

Happiness has to be cranked up;
trouble is a self-starter.

If only we'd stop trying to be happy,
we could have a pretty good time.
Edith Wharton

Most folks are about as happy as they
make up their minds to be.
Abraham Lincoln

Grief can take care of itself,
but to get the full value from joy, you
must have somebody to divide it with.
Mark Twain

IDENTITY

...grab some
for yourself.

Of course we categorize things–if we didn't, we'd have a hodge-podge of mental pictures and ideas aimlessly floating around in our head! Well, maybe some of us do anyway, but a few categories make sense. Tomato? Food. Car? Transportation.

And we choose a category for ourselves. If we're the self-satisfied sort, we might select Important. Influential. Powerful. If we're self-effacing, we'll hang our head and shuffle toward Ordinary. Insignificant. Nobody.

Either way, God has a category you can count on, and it's *His*. Yes, you belong to Him. Kind of makes all those other labels irrelevant, doesn't it?

Salute thyself;
see what thy soul doth wear.
George Herbert

If I knew myself, I'd run away.
Goethe

When a man is wrapped up in himself,
he makes a very small package.

I cannot think that we are useless
or God would not have created us.
Geronimo

When arguing with someone
you think is an idiot, make sure he isn't
doing the same thing.

We do not deal much in facts when we
are contemplating ourselves.
Mark Twain

The beginning of wisdom is to call things
by their right names.
Proverb

JOBS

...the paying kind and others.

Who's your boss? Even if it's the person frowning at you right now because you're reading instead of working, there's another boss who saw you first this morning. That's the one who stared at you in the bathroom mirror.

Only you can make your work fulfilling. Whether what you do takes place inside or outside the home, and whether you're paid in money or a pat on the back, real reward is something you give yourself.

You're the boss. Plan a great day, and other bosses won't seem so bad, even if they frown.

A job-seeker took an aptitude test the other day and found that he was best suited for retirement.

Work like a dog. Eat like a horse. Think like a fox. Run like a rabbit. Nap like a cat. And don't forget to visit your veterinarian for your yearly exam.

Those who know how to roll up their sleeves are rarely in danger of losing their shirt.

Unfortunately, she had to leave her position due to illness and fatigue. Her supervisor was sick and tired of her.

A college graduate was applying for a job, and the recruiter asked what kind of salary he was looking for. Deciding to go for it, the graduate confidently declared, "At least $175,000 to start."

"I see," said the recruiter, "and how about two months' vacation, free medical and dental, 100% company match for your 401(k) and a fully loaded company car?"

The graduate's eyes widened with glee. "Are you kidding?" he gasped.

"Of course," replied the recruiter, "but you started it."

KIDS

...you were one once, too, you know!

Just when we thought we had bent every rule while growing up, along comes the next generation to show us how it's *really* done! And if you wonder what they'll think of next, just stick around and you'll find out.

But while you're waiting, you might want to try something a little beyond the norm yourself. Turquoise and purple hair, anyone? Maybe or maybe not, but surely there's something you'd like to do…like wear an artsy outfit…hang out at a coffee shop…go to a rock concert… live, laugh…have fun.

Startle the kids.

Today, kids of four know all the
questions, and by fourteen they know
all the answers.

My son earns more now than I did on my
first job. What bothers me is that he's
seven years old and it's his allowance.

Being around kids is like having
a bowling alley in your brain.

Two boys acted up in Sunday school week after week until their teacher, at her wit's end, sent them to see the pastor. The first boy went in his office and sat down. The pastor said, "Son, do you know where God is?" The boy's jaw dropped, but he said nothing. Repeating his question, the pastor looked him directly in the eye and said, "Can you tell me where God is?" At that, the boy sprang from his chair, tore out of the office, and ran home. When his friend caught up with him, he asked the boy what had happened.

"God's missing," the panic-stricken lad reported, "and they think it's our fault!"

LAUGH
...it's like a
tickle from
the inside out!

Most of us don't laugh enough. Maybe we're influenced by the super-serious guy who walks around with a furrowed brow all the time. He must be thinking deep thoughts, right? Maybe, or maybe it's chronic indigestion.

The best way to manage the heavy things life sends us is to laugh–not at them, but despite them. Laughter lightens your mood, releases tension, and leaves you with the emotional energy you need to tackle everything serious.

Besides, all a furrowed brow will do is give you a pleated forehead.

Laugh and the world laughs with you;
cry and you have to blow your nose.

It's not a good idea to swallow laughter;
it goes back down to your hips.

We are all here for a spell;
get all the good laughs you can.
Will Rogers

Even if there's nothing to laugh at,
laugh on credit.

Mirth is God's medicine.
Everybody ought to bathe in it.
Henry Ward Beecher

Laughter is the shock absorber that
eases travel over the potholes of life.

Learn to laugh at yourself, and you'll
never be without something to laugh at.

You don't stop laughing
when you grow old; you grow old
when you stop laughing.

LIFE
...enjoy it now!

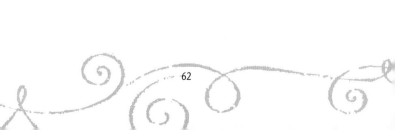

Living in the present is a little like standing on a balance bar. Yes, we're well aware of what's on either side of us–yesterday and tomorrow–but the center, today, commands our full concentration. That's where we want to keep our feet firmly planted.

God gave us life to live moment by moment. It seems pretty clear He's trying to tell us something about living each day as it comes–about walking attentively in the present, gracefully posed between our past and our future.

Never let yesterday
use up too much of today.
Will Rogers

Forever is composed of nows.
Emily Dickinson

One today is worth two tomorrows.
Benjamin Franklin

If you have one eye on yesterday
and one eye on tomorrow,
you're going to be cockeyed today.

The best thing about the future is that it
comes only one day at a time.
Abraham Lincoln

Kiss your life. Accept it, just as it is.
Today. Now. So that those moments
of happiness you're waiting for
don't pass you by.

MEMORIES

...blast from
the past.

You know how happy memories, even those decades old, still have the power to make you smile? Go ahead– think of one now for an instant facelift!

But if you like to feel the pull of gravity on your mouth muscles, start rifling through assorted unhappy recollections. They've got the same kind of power that happy memories do, and if you spend more than a second with them, your looks, mood, and attitude are sure to take a sharp dive downward.

If a blast from the past doesn't make you smile, it's a wind best blown back to yesterday.

When I was younger,
I could remember anything,
whether it had happened or not.
Mark Twain

People who have a clear conscience
probably also have a poor memory.

Remember being a teenager and trying
to look older? What were we thinking?

Write kindnesses in marble,
and write injuries in the dust.
Proverb

I used to have a photographic memory,
but now I think I'm running out of film.

A man, concerned about his memory, went to see the doctor about it. "I forget where I put things and where I'm supposed to be," the patient said. "And once I get there, I forget what I came for. In stores, I forget what I wanted to buy, and when I get to the cashier, I find I've forgotten my wallet. What can I do?"

"Hmmm," the doctor said as he thought over the symptoms. "To start, you will want to pay me in advance."

MONEY
**talks
...it says good-bye.**

A budget works if you have a magically funded category labeled Budget Busters. Items: repair for blown tire...patch for leaky roof...stitches for skinned knee.

But no matter how your budget looks at the end of the month, it can start out right at the beginning of the month. That's when Sharing is the category funded first. Items: support for your church...donation to your favorite charity...help for persons in need.

Sharing first may not prevent a Budget Buster later, but it keeps you spiritually funded to handle anything!

Money doesn't grow on trees;
you've got to beat the bushes for it.

The only thing you get free
of charge is a dead battery.

You have enough money
to last you for the rest of your life—
if you don't buy anything.

It's easy to meet expenses—
everywhere you go, there they are!

The arthritic contortionist was forced to
retire when he found he could no longer
make ends meet.

A couple was shipwrecked on a remote island. After weeks of waiting for rescue, the wife's thoughts turned toward home. "Honey," she asked, "did you pay the mortgage before we left?"

"Oh, I forgot," replied the husband.

"What about the car payment?" queried the wife.

"I'm sorry," came the response, "but that slipped my mind, too."

"The credit cards?"

"Those, too."

"And the store charge accounts?"

"Same," admitted the husband.

"Well, there's one good thing," the wife sighed. "They're sure to find us."

NEIGHBORS

...gotta love 'em!

Along with our relatives, we don't choose our neighbors. We move in, and there they are, to our left and right and across the street (at least until they move out).

Getting to know our neighbors takes effort, because everyone's busy with their own family, work, and activities. Yet it's a worthwhile endeavor, because getting to know those who live around us builds community and nurtures understanding between people.

Sound lofty? Not at all. Community and understanding begin right where you live.

Summer must be over. My neighbors just
returned my patio furniture.

For what do we live,
but to make sport for our neighbors
and laugh at them in our turn?
Jane Austen

My neighbors keep me broke—
they keep buying things I can't afford.

Love thy neighbor—
but don't pull down your hedge.
Benjamin Franklin

How much time he saves
who does not look to see what his
neighbor says or does or thinks.
Marcus Aurelius

Don't laugh when your
neighbor's oven is on fire.
Proverb

OPTIMISM
...it works.

Here's the case for optimism. First, you look and feel better when you're pondering positive thoughts. Second, if a situation isn't going your way, an optimistic frame of mind helps you find something about it you can work in your favor. Third, you don't know what the future will bring, so you may as well expect the best (you have a 50/50 chance of being right).

Finally, optimism differentiates you from other people, who seem to think pessimism puts them in the know. It doesn't, really. It just makes them glum.

Optimism: A cheerful frame of mind
that enables a tea kettle to sing even
though it's in hot water up to its nose.

Since the house is on fire,
let us warm ourselves.
Proverb

An optimist may see a light where there
is none, but why must the pessimist
always run to blow it out?
René Descartes

An optimist is the guy who goes out
fishing for Moby Dick in a rowboat,
equipped with a harpoon, jar of tartar
sauce, and slice of lemon.

An optimist is a fellow who believes a
housefly is looking for a way to get out.
George Jean Nathan

The optimist fell from the top floor of a
skyscraper. As he passed the tenth floor
he yelled, "So far, so good!"

Optimist: Day-dreamer
more elegantly spelled.
Mark Twain

If everything is looking rosy,
you've obviously overlooked something
really important.

PATH

...always
includes a puddle
(or two).

If you're of a certain age, you might remember the Sunday drive. That's when Dad piled the family in the station wagon and hit the road with no particular destination in mind. Yes, back then gas was cheap and smog hadn't yet turned the sky yellow!

But life without a destination isn't as carefree as a Sunday drive. Though there will be detours, and even sharp turns now and then, it helps to know where you're headed.

If you wonder which path to pick, or if you'd like help reading the signs along the way, ask God. He'll point you in the right direction.

Life is not about how fast you run,
or how high you climb,
but how well you bounce.

Even if you are on the right track,
you will get run over if you just sit there.
Will Rogers

Life is what we make it,
always has been, always will be.
Grandma Moses

Along this track of pathless ocean
it is my intention to steer.
Christopher Columbus

He considered himself an independent
thinker and always ready for adventure
and new experiences, a man willing to
take the road less traveled. His wife
called him a dunderhead for never
stopping and asking for directions.

PRAY

...bend God's
ear today.

If all else fails, read the instructions–and for many of us, it's the failure of every other option that leads us to prayer!

A prayer every morning gets you in the habit of involving God in your whole day, well before you reach your wit's end. It's like looking at the instructions before putting together that assemble-it-yourself bicycle. You'll be glad you did.

And if you still reach a desperation point later on, continue praying. You've already got hold of God's ear.

One Sunday morning, little Bobby told the minister that his mother prayed with him every night. Impressed, the minister asked him, "That's very good! And what does she say?"

"Always the same thing," Bobby replied. "Thank God he's in bed!"

The best wireless plan ever—Prayer.
Unlimited minutes! Unlimited messages!

The trouble with our praying is,
we just do it as a means of last resort.
Will Rogers

As long as there are algebra tests,
there will be prayer in public schools.

A day hemmed in prayer
won't ravel at the edges.

QUESTIONS

...ever wonder why?

Why do "Slow Children" signs show a picture of running children? Why is it called "rush hour" when no one's going over 5 mph? Why do we refer to nighttime as "after dark" when it's really "after light"?

And why leave all the curious questions to two-year-olds? They look at the world and all that's in it with brand-new eyes. Of course, they're two, so their eyes are brand new. But even those of us with not-so-new eyes can still blink and look again. And ask, "Why?"

But not incessantly, like a two-year-old. Maybe just think it.

I keep six honest serving-men
(They taught me all I knew);
Their names are What and Why and When
And How and Where and Who.
Rudyard Kipling

The census taker was going through the neighborhood door to door. Halfway down the block, he came to Mrs. Jones' house. When she answered his knock, he proceeded to go through his list of questions. She cooperated, except when it came to the question of her age. "But everyone else told their age," the census taker said.

"So," Mrs. Jones replied, "Did Helen Hill and Edith Hill next door tell you how old they are?"

"Yes, they did," he assured her.

"Then I'm the same age!"

"Okay," the census taker said putting pen to paper. "I'll put down 'old as the Hills.'"

REALITY
...sometimes bites.

A reality check can be about as pleasant as a root canal. Suddenly you're made aware of something everyone else has known for the past year and a half. Feels awful, doesn't it? (Just look at it this way: now you're in the loop.)

There are, however, good, positive, and productive reality checks. They not only keep you in the know, but also zap you with emotional strength and spiritual vitality. For instance, the reality of God's love for you is something you'll want to check out, and the more often the better. It's a reality check that's more than pleasant—it's downright joyous!

I think someone put a
"stop payment" on my reality check.

Few people have the
imagination for reality.
Goethe

Reality is that part of the imagination
we all agree on.

I have a very firm grasp on reality!
I can reach out and strangle it any time!

How many legs does a dog have if you
call the tail a leg? Four. Calling a tail a
leg doesn't make it a leg.
Abraham Lincoln

Reality can be beaten
with enough imagination.
Mark Twain

RISK

...sounds risky

You've heard of taking a "calculated" risk, but how exactly can you "calculate" a risk? The number-cruncher on your desktop (or on top of your desk) doesn't help when the risk can't be measured in dollars and cents, but in feelings and emotions.

It comes down to knowing what fits with your core principles and values... with where you see yourself, say, five years from now...with an eyes-wide-open analysis of what will benefit you and what will not.

Though unlike numbers that pop up on a calculator, this kind of risk calculation gives you answers you can count on.

Allow yourself to go on a
wild goose chase once in a while—
that's what wild geese are for.

I believe in getting into hot water;
it keeps you clean.
G. K. Chesterton

Don't be afraid to go out on a limb.
That's where the fruit is.

I dip my pen in the blackest ink, because
I'm not afraid of falling into my inkpot.
Ralph Waldo Emerson

The more chance there is of stubbing
your toe, the more chance you have of
running into opportunity.

The person who has had a bull by the tail
once has learned 60 to 70 times as much
as a person who hasn't.
Mark Twain

SILENCE
...yell if you love it!

"Silence is golden" in movie theaters, but it's not silent–those actors are making a lot of noise! If we really want racket-free space, we have to create it for ourselves.

An easy way is to walk out of the theater, go home, and turn off everything that makes noise–electronic things, that is. Dogs and small children are another matter.

The hard part (even with quiet dogs and children) is to silence our head chatter. Yap, yap, yap! Silence needs something to focus on–something meaningful enough to mute our inner yammering–someone like God.

He had occasional flashes of silence that
made his conversation perfectly delightful.
Sydney Smith

I have often lamented that we
cannot close our ears with as much ease
as we can our eyes.
Richard Steele

Never miss a good chance to shut up.
Will Rogers

Sitting in their "Boys Only" tree house, little Jimmy sobbed to his playmate, "My sister told me she won't talk to me for three whole weeks!"

"Wow, I'd be happy if my sister wouldn't talk to me for three weeks," his playmate said. "Why on earth are you crying?"

"Because today's the last day," Jimmy replied.

SUCCESS

...is what?

Success in life–what does it mean to you?

Many of us accept definitions offered by others, such as landing a plum position in a prestigious company, being famous, wielding power and influence over others. But are those things really what you'd come up with?

Put it to yourself this way: If you were to compare yourself to no one else in the world, then what would be your measure of success?

That's what success in life means to you, and you're the one that matters.

If at first you succeed,
try hard to hide your astonishment.
Harry F. Banks

Success gives some people big heads,
and other people big headaches.

Some people dream of success,
while others wake up and get to work.
Winston Churchill

Success comes in cans;
failures in can'ts.

You cannot climb the ladder of success
with your hands in your pockets.
Proverb

It's wise to remember that neither
success nor failure is permanent.
Roger Babson

I owe my success to having listened
respectfully to the very best advice,
and then going away and
doing the exact opposite.
G. K. Chesterton

TALK
…is expensive.

If you think talk is cheap, just look at your phone bill! But even before the age of top-tier plans with unlimited minutes, talk has never been cheap.

It takes only one offhand remark to impoverish a heart, ruin a reputation, or bankrupt a friendship. An opinion served up half-baked costs in embarrassment, and words released in anger are paid for with later regret.

Talk that helps, heals, entertains, praises, and encourages has a price tag, too. It's readily paid by putting the brain in gear before the mouth in motion.

Even a fish wouldn't get in trouble
if he would keep his mouth shut.

I don't have to attend
every argument I'm invited to.

Life is far too important a thing
ever to talk seriously about.
Oscar Wilde

The pastor's sermon was like God's love—
it was beyond understanding
and utterly without end.

It's really annoying when people keep
talking while I'm interrupting.

It usually takes me more than three
weeks to prepare a
good impromptu speech.
Mark Twain

I am so clever that sometimes
I don't understand a single word
of what I am saying.
Oscar Wilde

I wish my mouth had a delete key.

TRUTH
...isn't easy.

Do these jeans make by hips look big? Isn't it obvious my little Billy is brilliant? Can you believe the whopper that got away? Some questions you just don't want to answer!

But when someone we care about is on a dangerous course, our love for the person compels us to speak up. Even if she takes offense, at least we know the person has heard the truth.

In the same way, God tells us the truth because He cares about us. Even if His truth should upset, disturb, or offend us, God's truth is what we need to hear.

Always do right! This will gratify some
people and astonish the rest.
Mark Twain

The trouble with stretching the truth is
that it's likely to snap back at you.
Proverb

A lie has traveled around the world before
Truth has gotten her boots on.

The fisherman, just back from a day on the lake, couldn't wait to tell his buddy about the fish he had hooked. He described his adventure in great detail. After many gyrations to indicate the fish's weight and strength, and throwing his arms open as wide as they would go to suggest its size, he declared, "Why, I've never seen such a fish!"

"That," his friend replied, "is something I can believe."

UNCERTAINTY

...not sure
about it.

It's hard to get comfortable with uncertainty. Most of us crave knowing exactly what will happen next and how things will turn out, and yet we never do. We might be 99.99% sure based on probabilities, but without-a-doubt certain? Nope!

Trust in God's care helps us live with uncertainty, because no matter what happens, we can rely on His constant presence and care for us. When we acknowledge His control over all, we can accept life's hidden mysteries…such as what tomorrow will bring. It's okay.

With God, we can cope with surprises.

I know nothing with any certainty, but the
sight of the stars makes me dream.
Vincent Van Gogh

Every generalization is dangerous,
especially this one.
Mark Twain

The grand perhaps! We look on helplessly,
there the old misgivings,
crooked questions are.
Robert Browning

Tell a man there are 300 billion stars in
the universe, and he'll believe you.
Tell him a bench has wet paint on it,
and he'll have to touch it to be sure.
Murphy's Law

Uncertainty and expectation
are the joys of life.
William Congreve

Who knows nothing, doubts nothing.
Proverb

If the Sun and Moon should doubt,
they'd immediately go out.
William Blake

VALUES

...it's good to
have some.

Ever seen a tumbleweed caught up in a whirlwind? The bramble bounces and spins until dropped, maybe a mile or two away. You can imagine the tumbleweed waking up and wondering what happened!

If we're not committed to a clear set of solid values, we're much like the hapless tumbleweed. When winds of excitement, emotion, fear, or compulsion blow, we're caught up in the current, taken on a dizzying ride, and dropped far from where we thought we were.

Values are the roots that keep us planted where we want to be...and as the person we want to become.

A man is usually more careful of his
money than he is of his principles.
Ralph Waldo Emerson

You can out-distance that which
is running after you, but not what
is running inside you.
Proverb

Live in such a way that you would
not be ashamed to sell your parrot
to the town gossip.
Will Rogers

Character is much easier
kept than recovered.
Thomas Paine

Do not do or say anything you wouldn't
sign your name to.

My goal in life is to be as good of a
person as my dog thinks I am.

WISDOM

...so you want to be a wise guy?

Did you hear the one about the dolt who bought an AM radio? It took him a week before he realized he could play it at night!

Wise guys (and gals) are those who take on the day with a full load of common sense (which, by the way, is not so common). And common sense isn't out of reach–it's just a matter, most often, of being willing to step back and think before reaching a conclusion.

About radios. About work. About other people. About life.

Those who are wise can see more from
the bottom of a well than a fool can
from a mountain top.

Be happy. It's one way of being wise.
Colette

I do not think much of a man who is not
wiser today than he was yesterday.
Abraham Lincoln

Common sense in an uncommon degree is
what the world calls wisdom.
Coleridge

A single conversation with a wise man is
better than ten years of study.
Proverb

If you're wise, resign as general
manager of the universe.

WIT
...why, how clever of you!

Some people seem born with the ability to come up with a witty remark at a moment's notice. Their twinkling eyes let everyone know their words are in jest, and the laughter brings hearers together instantly in an atmosphere of warmth and friendliness.

And then there's the rest of us. Hours after everyone's gone home, the perfect line pops into our head. Sigh.

A kindly heart and love for others is fertile soil for wit that warms, invigorates, and refreshes. It's also the perfect ground to stand on as an appreciative audience for those who make us laugh.

An original wit is the guy who hears the
gag before you do.

Many a true word was spoken in jest.
Proverb

Brevity is the soul of wit.
William Shakespeare

Wit is the salt of conversation,
not the food.
William Hazlitt

Every survival kit should
include a sense of humor.

The greatest advantage I know of
being thought a wit by the world
is that it gives one the greater freedom
of playing the fool.
Alexander Pope

XO XO XO

...aw, shucks!

"It's love that makes the world go round" says the song lyrics. While love may not be responsible for the rotation of Earth on its axis, it certainly makes our relationships on Earth meaningful and fulfilling.

For love to do its work in our life, however, it has to come from within. Not one of us can truly love others, or happily embrace the love of others, unless we first love ourselves.

Love yourself, because God loves you. If you wonder how much, just ask Him. It will make your world go 'round.

Kisses are always sweeter than whine.

Love means nothing in tennis,
but it's everything in life.

To the world, you might be one person;
but to one person,
you might be the world.

A kiss without a hug is like a flower
without the fragrance.
Proverb

Anyone can catch your eye, but it takes
someone special to touch your heart.

The heart that loves is always young.
Proverb

YOUNG AT HEART

...right now.

It's never too early to start being young at heart! Why leave all the joys of a youthful perspective to those 90 years old and up?

You're not too young (or too old) to take a tip from those who have found that attitude isn't dependent on age, appearance, health, or ability. Your attitude about life depends on choices you make–the negative thoughts you toss out of your mind, and the positive ones you gather in.

A young-at-heart outlook is what you want at any age!

You're only young once,
but you can be immature forever.

Birthdays are nice, but too many of them
certainly ages a person.

Life would be infinitely happier if we
could only be born at the age of eighty and
gradually approach eighteen.
Mark Twain.

I don't have a problem with getting older,
but my body's having real issues with it.

None are so old as those who
have outlived enthusiasm.
Thoreau

A facelift might take ten years
off your looks, but it won't do anything
for climbing a flight of stairs.

Here's the secret to eternal youth—
lie about your age.

ZEST

...an ap*peel*ing approach to life!

Zest for life—you know it when you see it! It's energetic, enthusiastic, and alive in a way that's infectious. Ever notice how animated, upbeat people make everyone around them feel more vibrant?

If you're not radiating zest for life right now, that's okay. You need down time, too. But when you're ready to get up, how about this? Name something you really enjoy doing...care about deeply...believe is truly important...and do it.

Give it all you've got. You'll feel great, and you just might inspire someone you love to get up off the couch and start living!

Mirth is the sweet wine of human life.
It should be offered sparkling
with zestful life unto God.
Henry Ward Beecher

Enthusiasm isn't automatic—
it must be nurtured.

It's faith in something and enthusiasm for
something that makes a life worth living.
Oliver Wendell Holmes